ON THE PISTE

CHAMELEON

First published in Great Britain in 1999 by

Chameleon Books

76 Dean Street

London W1V 5HA

Copyright for text © Generation Publications Ltd

CIP data for this title is available from the British Library

ISBN 0 233 99497 1

Book and jacket design by Generation Studio

Origination by Digicol London

Printed in Spain

André Deutsch Ltd is a VCI plc company

ACKNOWLEDGEMENTS:

Also a special thanks to Dave Crowe, Eddie Schillace,

Paul Sudbury, Linda Baritski, Caroline Warde, Eve Cossins, Mark Peacock,

Mary Killingworth, Joe Crowe, Louise Edwards and Tim Forrester.

PHOTOGRAPH ACKNOWLEDGEMENTS

All Photographs supplied by Allsport U.K LTD.

EAGLE DROP-INS!

I think that skiing is the most exciting thing that you can do with your clothes on!!

I have been skiing for 21 years and I am just as excited to put my skis on now as when I first started when I was 13 years old.

Now it's easier than ever to start skiing, most Schools, Colleges or Youth groups organise ski trips and with Plastic Ski Slopes in most parts of the country it's relatively easy to book a lesson and have a go.

One thing has definitely changed, the Ski instructors have got prettier. When I had my first lessons the Ski Instructors were huge, hairy and looked like Russian Shot-putters... and they were just the women!!

My first ski trip was with the school to Andalo in the Italian Dolomites it was fantastic, I loved every minute of it. I did my first ski jump there after only four days on skis. I found myself hurtling at great speed down towards the bottom of a blue run, there was a single track road in front of me, I hadn't quite mastered how to stop yet and I hit a bank of snow, went flying through the air over the road, over a wooden fence and into someone's back garden, it could have been my first British record!!

I started skiing regularly at Gloucester Ski Centre where I eventually learned how to stop as well as turn to the left and right...which can be quite useful when skiing!!

My skiing went from strength to strength and my jumps got longer too. I started jumping over my friends on a weekly basis, I eventually jumped over 30 people in a row, with my best friends at the front of the course, before moving onto the hard stuff...cars, trucks and buses!!

My first jump over a car was a bit of an accident. I was planning to jump off the bottom of the ski slope at Gloucester, over a grass bank, over a wire fence and into the Car-Park. I skied down the slope at great speed towards the bottom of the slope but unfortunately I hit the end of the slope at the wrong angle. I still cleared the grass bank and the wire fence, I also cleared the bright red BMW that was parked in the car park!!

Luckily enough I have never hit any of the cars, buses or trucks that I have jumped over but I did hit one of my friends once, it was his fault though, he moved and stood in exactly the same place as I was planning to land. No serious damage done though he was out of hospital after a few days!!

I have had a few scrapes in my time, but then I have also had a few lucky breaks, the luckiest one of all was when I was 17 years old and working in Colle di Tenda ski resort in Italy. I was challenged to race the local ski champion called Nino from the top of the mountain to the bottom and it was decided that the winner would take out to dinner a five foot ten blonde bombshell named June. On a cold Wednesday morning we both launches ourselves from the top of the hill, racing towards the bottom Nino was just ahead of me so I took this bend slightly sharper than him, suddenly I was thrown into the air and I came down on top of Nino. We were both travelling at around 75 mph. I bounced off him and hit a tree. I was taken to hospital with a broken neck and back and was put in traction for three weeks. In the meantime Nino took June out to dinner. I was eventually released from hospital after a month in agony but I was very lucky because Nino went on to marry June a year later and has been in agony ever since!!

I didn't start jumping until I was 22 years old and although I started in the USA I did a lot of my jumping in a tiny village called Kandersteg in Switzerland. I was using very old equipment that included a helmet that was only attached to me by a piece of string. One day I was jumping on the 90 metre jumping hill. Sliding down towards take-off, I launched myself into the air but I put so much force into the take-off that the string snapped on my helmet and as I was flying through the air my helmet fell off. Do you know it was the biggest mistake of my life. I should have held on to that helmet because I jumped 36 metres but my helmet jumped 86...and it had better style!!!

I can't go without giving my fellow skiers and potential skiers a ski tip, so my very important ski tip to you all is...don't eat yellow snow!!

Eddie 'The Eagle' Edwards.

Can we come, too?

Although skating and ice hockey had
previously been part of the Summer
Olympic Games programme, the first
Winter Olympics were staged in 1924.
Initially called "International Sports
Week", the event was retitled the
Winter Games a couple of years later
in 1926.

Seventeen nations took part in the
opening ceremony, but only 16 of
them actually competed in the Games
themselves – for some reason Estonia
enjoyed the opening party but didn't
actually bring any competitors along.

6

Long wait for a medal

In the 1924 Winter Games Norwegian skier Thorleif Haug finished with a haul of three gold medals and also a bronze in a special jumping event. Some 50 years later, though, a Norwegian sports historian discovered that the points tally had been incorrectly calculated, and it was actually Anders Haugen, a Norwegian-American, who had come third, not fourth, as originally stated. In 1974, the bronze medal given to Thorleif Haug was handed on to the 86-year-old Haugen by Haug's daughter.

"HILDE, STOP SHAKING YOUR HEAD, THERE'S DANDRUFF EVERYWHERE."

Referee!

Bad weather dogged the 1928 Winter Olympics at St Moritz. Some events were curtailed, and controversy abounded in the 10,000 metre skating event when the Norwegian referee lost any American friends that he had won in the 1920 Summer Olympics.

That's not ladylike

Theresa Weld of the USA was one of the first female ice skaters to incorporate jumps into a figure-skating programme in 1920. It didn't go down too well with the Olympic judges, however. They reprimanded Weld for displaying unfeminine behaviour.

Golden skates

Norway's Sonja Henie won three consecutive gold medals in the Winter Games, winning the figure-skating event in 1928, 1932 and 1936. She had actually competed in the 1924 Games as well, at the tender age of 11. Henie went on to turn professional and reaped the reward from ice dancing shows and films to the tune of some $47 million in earnings .

'WHO LET THE BLOODY TRUCK ON THE RUN.'

Bobless

The 1960 Winter Games at the purpose-built Squaw Valley complex in the USA lacked a bobsled run as the organisers had refused to take on the additional cost of construction for something they regarded as an insignificant event.

Drugged up

The Soviet Nordic skier Gakina Kulakova was disqualified from her third place finish in the 5000m event in 1976 because she was found to be using a banned substance. To combat the flu bug which affected many athletes, Kulakova was using a nasal spray which was found to contain an illegal drug. Bizarrely, Kulakova was still allowed to compete in other events and actually ended up winning a gold and a bronze.

Crowd pleasers

The 1952 Winter Games in Oslo were rated a huge success for spectators. The ski jumping event was watched by something in the region of 150,000 people.

Show-off

Norwegian skier Bjorn Dahlie had a successful 1992 Games, winning three gold medals and a silver. His third gold came in the relay event, and to celebrate victory Dahlie crossed the winning line skiing backwards.

"IF YOU CAN'T BEAT THEM IN THE ALLEY, YOU CAN'T BEAT THEM ON THE ICE."
Ice hockey player Punch I

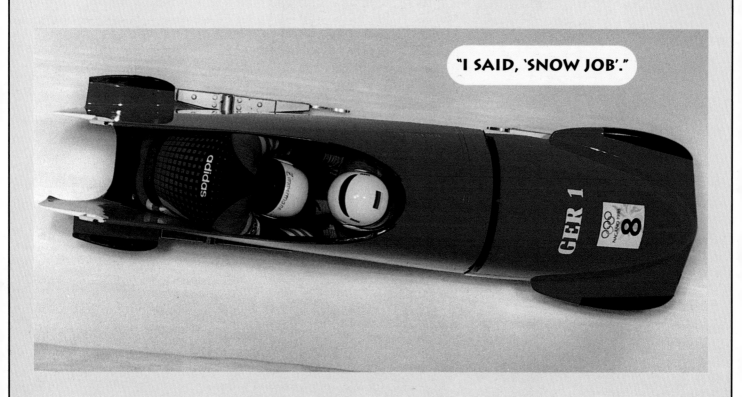

"I SAID, 'SNOW JOB'."

One at a time, please

Ice hockey was the centre of controversy in the 1948 Winter Games as the USA turned up with two teams. One of the teams represented the Amateur Hockey Association (AHA) of the USA, while the other was the selection of the US Olympic Committee.

The AHA team was a member of the International Hockey Federation which threatened to withdraw all its member teams if the US AHA team was barred from playing. The US Olympic Committee, on the other hand, said it would withdraw its entire American Olympic team if its hockey players were not allowed to compete. In the end the organisers deemed that only the AHA team would play representing the USA, and they finished fourth.

"BOLLOCKS, MY SKIS ARE STUCK."

First post

German postman Georg Thoma won gold in the 1960 Nordic skiing event, saying that completing his daily mail round in the snow at home had helped him train for the event.

I want to work with children

Jeanette Altwegg won Britain's first gold medal in a skating event for 44 years by taking first place in the ladies' figure skating in the 1952 Winter Games. Altwegg was one of the few successful figure skaters to spurn the potential riches of professionalism and instead went to work in the Swiss village for orphan children, Pestalozzi.

IRISH
SNOWBOARDER

Now all hold hands as we cross the line...

The 500 metre speed skating race in the 1928 Winter Games saw an uncommon occurrence. Two men tied in first place and three more finished level behind them. The result was the awarding of two gold medals and three bronze, but no silver.

Presidential bobsled

Eleanor Roosevelt, wife of President Franklin D Roosevelt who officially opened the 1932 Games, enjoyed her outing to Lake Placid so much that she even volunteered to take a run down the bobsled course. There is no record of what the First Lady's bob time was.

"MR. GRIMSDALE!"

First corner chaos

Before 1932 Europeans had traditionally dominated the speed-skating events, but the Americans, enjoying home advantage, changed the rules of the event to favour themselves and the Canadian competitors. Instead of racing in pairs and awarding medals on the fastest times, as happened in Europe, the 1932 Games saw mass start races, exactly as happens in middle- and long-distance running on the track. Unfamiliar with the tactics and aggression needed to compete in this manner, the Europeans were simply, and sometimes almost literally, brushed aside.

"IS FART PROPULSION ALLOWED?"

Jacob's cracker

The 1924 Winter Games ski-jump champion, Jacob Tullin-Thams of Norway, not only successfully defended his title in 1928 (a massive jump of 73 metres saw him run out of landing space) but he also cropped up in the 1936 Summer Games to win a silver medal in yachting.

Duty-free snow

An unseasonable spell of warm weather meant that snow for the 1932 Winter Games in Lake Placid, USA, had to be brought in from across the border in Canada.

Smile!

Gillis Grafstrom of Sweden saw his chances of winning four consecutive titles in figure skating dashed when he managed to collide with a film camera recording the event. Grafstrom suffered concussion, but at least he got a good close-up in.

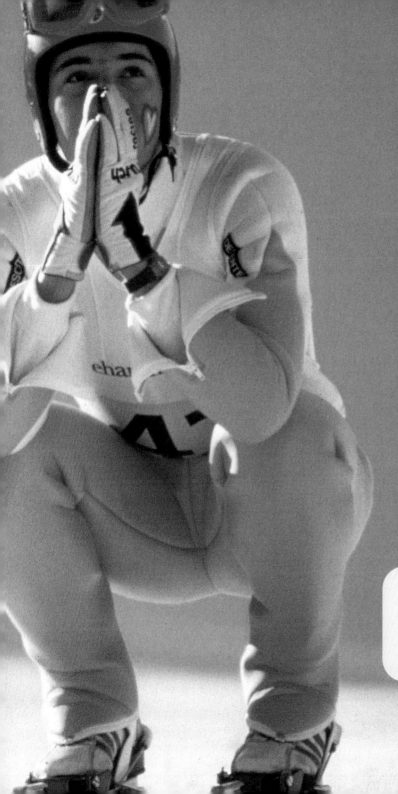

Spoil-sports

The 1994 Olympics saw a crackdown on skimpy, revealing costumes in the figure-skating competition, much to the chagrin of the sell-out crowds.

Sister act

The 1968 Olympic women's slalom was won by French skier Marielle Goitschel, thus emulating the success her sister had enjoyed at the previous Winter Games in 1964.

"LET'S SEE, WHAT IS THE BEST SHAG I EVER HAD....."

The reserve was an accountant

The 1932 four-man bob team from the USA was an interesting bunch of characters. Lead man Fiske was the first American pilot to join the RAF and was killed in the Battle of Britain. Second man O'Brien married Hollywood silent-film star Mae Murray. Clifford Gray was a songwriter and his biggest tune was "If you were the only girl in the world." Finally, fourth man Eddie Egan was a 1920 Olympic gold medallist in boxing.

"NO! I DON'T WANT TO BE DRIVER."

"IT'S NOT AS NICE
AS HILLINGDON
SKI SLOPES."

"COO-EE, BOYS, I'M OVER HERE."

Is that a logo?

At the 1968 Winter Games the International Olympic Committee attempted to stem what it perceived as rampant commercialism by banning the showing of trade and brand names on a competitor's equipment. Some of the top skiers threatened to withdraw at such a draconian decree, and the IOC relented to the extent that it was agreed that brand names would not be visible on TV or in photographs.

FERGIE'S SKI
INSTRUCTOR

BETTER TRY THE CAT WALK

THE INVISIBLE MAN SNOW BOARDING.

Happy family

American couple Mr and Mrs Stevens
were proud parents in the 1932 Winter
Games. They had three sons competing
in the US team. Curtis and Hubert
paired up to win the two-man bobsled,
while Paul took home a silver medal
from the four-man event. They must
have been hell in their prams!

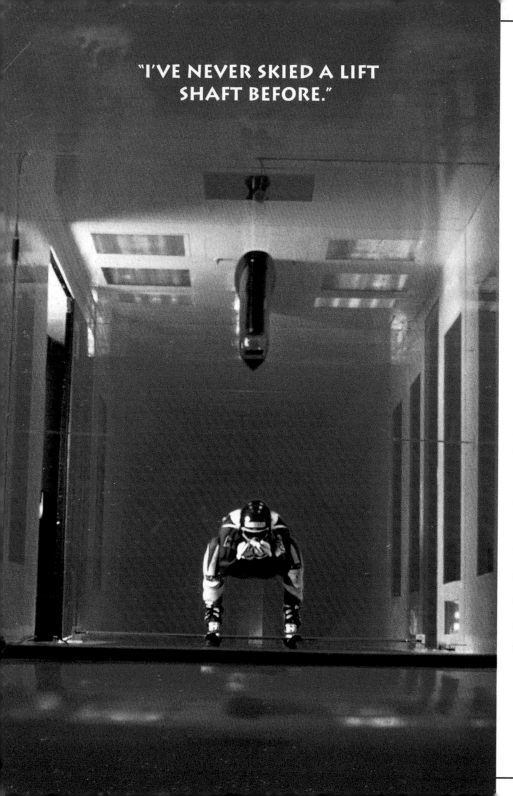

"I'VE NEVER SKIED A LIFT SHAFT BEFORE."

It's OK, nobody saw.

In 1956, at the traditional opening ceremony of the Winter Olympics, with the torch carried into the arena by a relay of runners, last-leg torch carrier Guido Carlo nearly suffered the ultimate embarrassment. As Carlo completed his circuit of the arena he tripped over and fell to the ground. Fortunately, the flame did not go out.

A little bit of Beethoven

The two nations of East and West Germany actually competed as one team in the 1960 Winter Games. Rather than one national anthem taking precedence over the other, they selected Beethoven's Ninth Symphony as the music to be played at any victory ceremonies - of which there were four that year.

Hot stuff

The East German women's luge team for the 1968 Games thought they had put the heat on their competitors by finishing first, second and fourth. It was discovered that the heat was directed at themselves, though, or more accurately at their sleds. In order to run faster, the German women had heated the sled runners, and were therefore disqualified.

Fair play indeed

Great Britain won bobsled gold at the 1964 Winter Games - the first country without an actual bob run of its own to do so. The British two man team owed some of their success to the sporting actions of Italian competitor Eugenio Monti who, after completing his own run, helped repair the British bob by taking the axle off his own bobsled and using it to replace the broken British axle. Monti received a Fair Play trophy for his deeds and got his just reward in 1968 by winning both olympic bobsled events. He was 40 years old.

Aaaaaagh!

The 70m ski-jump at the 1980 Olympics was deemed to be too dangerous after nine competitors had made their first jump, and indications were that there was not enough landing room for a safe finish. Rather than risk losing a few jumpers in the trees, officials moved the start point down the hill to reduce take-off speed and started the event again.

How much?

The Winter Games returned to Lake Placid, USA, in 1980, 48 years after the Games were first staged there. Things proved a mite more expensive second time around, though. In 1932 just over $1 million was spent on construction, in 1980 that figure was over $80m.

Sister act

The 1968 Olympic women's slalom was won by French skier Marielle Goitschel, thus emulating the success her sister had enjoyed at the previous Winter Games in 1964.

Head and shoulders above the rest

Australian skier Sam Guss certainly stood out in the 1984 Winter Games-he was six feet eight inches tall!

Momentum is everything

German luge competitor Hans Staggassinger may have had an unfair advantage in gaining speed when hurtling his sled downhill - he weighed in at nearly 17 and a half stone.

"THE BOARD SHOULD BE STRAPPED W-H-E-R-E.......!"

Bob and boxer

Eddie Egan was brought into the 1932 American four-man bobsled team at very late notice but still helped his crew to win the gold medal. The Winter Games medal no doubt looked very good in Egan's trophy cabinet next to the gold medal for boxing that he won in the 1920 Summer Olympics.

THE VINDALOO TECHNIQUE.
IT DOESN'T WORK.

"I'M SURE THESE AREN'T REAL BINOCULARS."

Super Hubers

Mr and Mrs Huber of Italy, take a bow. Their four sons all took part in the 1994 Winter Games. Wilfried and Norbert won gold and silver in the luge, Gunther won a bronze in the two-man bobsled and Arnold finished fourth in the luge singles race.

Gone to the dogs

Canada are the reigning champions in the Olympic event of dog-sled racing, and have held that honour since 1932, the one and only time dog-sled racing has been included in the Winter Games. For the record, Emile St Goddard piloted his team to victory in both the 25 mile races to take first place easily.

LETHAL WEAPON 3 1/2

Fast progress

The first Olympic Alpine Skiing event was held in 1936 and the first gold medal was claimed by Norwegian Birger Ruud, who also won the ski-jump. Ruud's downhill speed in winning the event, though, would rank him as a mere pedestrian in modern times. Ruud attained an average speed of 47.599km/h - compare that to American Bill Johnson's winning speed in 1984 when he averaged 104.532km/h.

A long wait for another go

In 1992 Speed Skiing was a demonstration event at the Olympics and representing Britain was Davina Galica, at the age of 47. This was not Galica's first Olympic appearance, however. She had also represented her country in Alpine Skiing, some 28 years previously.

GUESS WHO HAD BEANS ON TOAST FOR BREAKFAST

A weighty issue

Basic physics says that the heavier the weight put into a vehicle, the faster it will move down a slope. The German team figured this out for the four-man bobsled in 1952, piling their four biggest blokes into one sled to win easily. The average weight of the crew was 18 and a half stone. Rules governing weight limits on bobsleds and their crews were introduced shortly after.

Soap

Complicated intimate relations were the talk of the Russian ice-skating team in the early 1970s. Irina Rodnina and Aleksey Ulanov struck gold at the 1972 Winter Games in the figure-skating pairs, but Ulanov only had eyes for Ludmilla Smirnova, who had teamed up with Andrey Suraikin to win the silver medal. Rodnina and Ulanov split as a partnership because of the affair between Ulanov and Smirnova, who later got married. Rodnina, meanwhile, teamed up with Aleksandr Zaitsev, on the ice and between the sheets - they also got married and also won two Olympic titles as a figure-skating team. Confused???

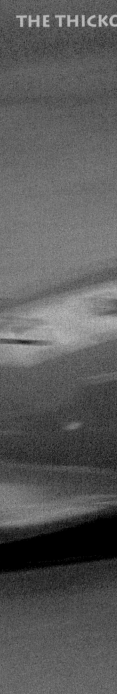

Shot stopper

American ice hockey goal keeper James Craig earned himself hero status in 1980 as his country won only its second gold medal in the event. Throughout the tournament Craig achieved an amazing statistic of saving over 90% of the shots directed at his goal. The figures show that Craig kept out 163 of 178 shots on target, including 39 in the match against the Soviet Union alone.

It takes a long time to make a decision

Curling was first seen at the Olympics as a demonstration sport in the 1924 Games - Great Britain winning a three-country tournament. But it wasn't until 1998 that the sport finally gained recognition as an official Olympic event.

Who needs a national team?

The first Olympic ice hockey champions were not a national Canadian side but rather the country's leading club side. Hence the reason why the Winnipeg Falcons skated their way into the history books in 1920.

"DON'T ANYONE FART!"

Help from above?

Jimmy "The Parson" Foster, so called because he contemplated entering the Church for a career at one time, was probably ice hockey's greatest goalminder of the 1930s. In a four year stretch with Moncton Hawks in Canada he missed only one of the 220 matches played by the team and saved an estimated 6,000 shots. At one stage he held the Canadian record of playing for a total of 417 minutes without conceding a goal. All this after breaking his leg in two places in 1930 and being told he might never play again.

Dedication or stupidity?

You've got to admire Austrian ski-jumper Sepp Bradl's persistence. He represented his country at the event for 20 years, from the 1936 Winter Games to the 1956 event. Despite being the first man to break 100 metres with a jump, he never actually won an Olympic medal.

FLY THE FLAG.

Auntie makes a mess of things

The BBC radio commentary of the deciding match in the 1936 Winter Games ice hockey between Great Britain and USA provoked outrage among spellbound listeners as the BBC pulled the plug on coverage before the end.

The match was finely balanced at 0-0 and was deep into overtime, causing the BBC to overrun by 45 minutes and therefore not only delay the news but scrap a piano recital.

The Beeb received a flood of complaints about their decision to leave the game before the final whistle, principally because if Great Britain had held on to the draw they would almost certainly secure the Olympic title. As it turned out the BBC missed the scoop, Britain held out and came home champions.

Ice roots

Who played the first ever game of ice hockey? It is a matter of some dispute between the Canadian cities of Kingston, Ontario and Montreal, Quebec. The people of Montreal say the first game was played in 1879 after a university student returned from a trip to England and looked to adapt the game of field hockey, which he had enjoyed on his trip, to ice.

Residents of Kingston, however, claim that the Royal Canadian Rifle regiment cleared the ice over Kingston harbour of snow and played a game of hockey on it as early as 1867.

But it could date as far back as medieval times when skating took place on the Fens in England and records suggest that some form of ice hockey may have been played.

"THERE IT IS."

Royal performance

In 1895, with the lake at Buckingham Palace frozen over, the Palace put out an ice hockey team to play a Canadian-led team. The Palace team included the Prince of Wales, who later took the throne as King Edward VII, and the Duke of York, who also eventually ascended to the throne as King George V. The Palace team was well beaten.

Scots stuffed

The first ice hockey international between England and Scotland was played in 1910 and resulted in a resounding English victory, 11-1.

Call this a Championship?

The 1921 European Championships for ice hockey were a somewhat farcical affair. Staged in Stockholm, the Swedes won the title on their home soil. But it wasn't an overly difficult achievement there was only one other country competing.

Cambridge blues

The first official ice hockey match outside Canada was played between Cambridge and Oxford Universities at St Moritz in 1885. Oxford won 6-0.

DON'T HAVE A CURRY
ON RACE DAY.

Say Cheese 1

In search of a better snapshot of the skiers coming down the Garmisch course during the 1997 downhill World Cup event, a spectator jumped the safety barriers and attempted to venture nearer the track. Unfortunately he slipped and slid uncontrollably into a landing zone for one of the course's jumps. Italian downhiller Pietro Vitalini was hurtling towards that point but somehow managed to hit the brakes and come to a halt before he caused a serious injury.

While the spectator hot-footed it into the forest to escape the long arm of the law, Vitalini was helicoptered back up to the starting line, recommenced his run, and recorded a time fast enough to finish in second place.

Say Cheese 2

Swedish speed skater Ake Seyffarth, a world-record holder in the 5000m event, was denied a gold medal at the 1948 Olympics thanks to a brush with a photographer - literally. Closing in on the coveted gold medal spot, Seyffarth collided with a photographer who had wandered on to the ice to get a decent close-up. He got closer than he anticipated, and the tangle cost Seyffarth precious seconds and he ended up in 8th place. Some consolation was that he later won gold in the 10,000m.

"THIS WASN'T IN THE TRAVEL BROCHURE."

Never take the wife to the match

Mrs Janet Gretsky, wife of ice hockey legend Wayne, came a cropper during a match between her husband's New York Rangers team and Chicago. Actress Janet, who starred in the unforgettable *Police Academy 5*, was knocked unconscious when a pane of Plexiglas, which separates the supporters from the rink, fell away from its frame after Chicago's Sergei Krvokrasov was body-checked into it.

Damn!

Dutch speed skater Ard Schenk couldn't have enjoyed more contrasting emotions at the 1972 Olympics. Schenk was the conqueror of allcomers in every race except one, over the shortest distance, 500 metres. But Schenk didn't even get close to the 500. Pushing off for his start, Schenk completed four steps before falling flat on his face. He finished 34th.

One-man band

Australia entered a team into the 1936 Winter Olympics. It wasn't a large team though, consisting of just one man, Ken Kennedy, a champion speed- skater and ice hockey player with the Birmingham Maple Leafs.

Slippery Dan

American speedskater Dan Jansen won gold at the 1994 Olympics in the 1000m, his only Olympic medal. He should have had more than that. Jansen came to the 1988 Olympics as the reigning world champion and firm favourite for the 500m title. He fell at the first bend. A few days later in the 1000m race he slipped over again. Worse was to follow. At the 1994 Olympics he managed to slip up again in the 500m race and only finished 8th. But thankfully he got that 1000m title safely in the bag before the Games were up.

Bum Note

British ice skater Celia Colledge could have won the 1936 Olympic gold medal, but was denied by bizarre circumstances. As she stepped on-to the ice to start her routine, the music commenced, but it was the wrong tune. Some frantic searching for the right music ensued, and when she finally started her routine, a flustered Colledge nearly fell over inside the first minute. She finished second overall.

True love

Dog-sled racer Dee Dee Jonrowe saw her opportunity to win the 500 mile Beargrease Dog-sled Marathon dashed by the course of true love. She decided to give her team of huskies a rest during the race, but two of the team felt they had enough energy left to make the most of the chance to further their relationship. The time Jonrowe lost in trying to separate the two lovedogs cost her any chance of winning the race.

A blow for women's rights

In the 1902 World Championships for Figure Skating, Britain's top female skater Madge Syers caused something of a rumpus by not only entering the Championships, which were effectively a male preserve, but by also finishing second to Sweden's Ulrich Salchow.

"THIS IS SLIPPERY AS ICE."
"IT IS ICE YOU IDIOT."

WHERE OLD
SKIERS GO TO DIE.

Well, it was Wimbledon v Crystal Palace

Danish sports fans appear to be turning away from football. A recent international Curling tournament attracted a far greater TV audience than the same evening's televised action from the English Premier League.

Man's golf

The most southerly golf course in the world is the Scott Base Country Club, located a mere 13 degrees north of the South Pole. Players need to wear full survival kit for their game, and course hazards include penguins, seals and skuas. A player is penalized one shot if his ball is stolen by a skua, but he can mark a birdie on his card should he manage to hit one.

Doh!

Britain's Alan Hinkes stumbled somewhat in his attempt to become the first British mountaineer to climb the world's 14 mountains measuring above 8000m. With base camp set up on the 26,000ft Nanga Parbat climb, Hinkes settled down to a nice chapati to assuage his hunger. It was a floury chapati, so floury in fact that it tickled his nose and made him sneeze. Unfortunately, the sneeze caused Hinkes to slip a disc in his back, and he had to crawl back down the mountain to seek rescue.

Official abuse

The Nottingham Panthers ice hockey team sacked their stadium organist after he first played 'Send In The Clowns' to greet the match officials as they came on to the rink, and then followed up with 'Three Blind Mice' as they left the arena when the match was over.

THE BLUE RUN

This is a stick-up

A group of Polish car-jackers picked on the wrong men when they forced Konstantin Vaigin and Gennady Ramensky off the road, because Vaigin was the coach of the Belarussian biathlon team and Ramensky was his Russian counterpart.

The two were returning from the world championships in Slovakia when the car-jackers struck. But the two coaches merely played for time while their respective squads of athletes caught up in their own transport. As the biathlon combines cross-country skiing and shooting, the car-jacking gang quite sensibly fled when the coach party tumbled out with rifles loaded.

Nobbled knee

Back in 1994, two American female ice-skaters held centre stage in the sporting headlines. Tonya Harding and Nancy Kerrigan were the stars of a bizarre drama surrounding this normally genteel sport. Kerrigan's appearance at the Winter Olympics that year was put in doubt after she was attacked by a man with a tyre iron and whacked on the knee. It transpired that Harding knew the attacker, and indeed had full knowledge of the planned attack. She was found guilty of conspiracy and fined $160,000 as well as being banned for life. Kerrigan still competed in the Games and almost won gold, but had to settle for second place by the slimmest of margins. Harding finished eighth.

Simpson's escape

When mountaineer Simon Yates attempted to rescue his climbing partner Joe Simpson, who had crashed through a crevasse, he found that he simply did not have the energy to haul Simpson back to safety. He either had to cut the rope or die along with his partner, so he cut the rope and Simpson plummeted into blackness. Frostbitten and exhausted, Yates trekked back to camp, overcome with remorse. But Simpson wasn't finished. He survived the fall with a broken leg, but crawled, hopped and dragged himself back to the camp. It took him six days without food or *water*. When he got back, his first words to Yates were: "Thanks, Simon. You did right."

HE SHOULD HAVE USED HEAD AND SHOULDERS.

Starting fast

Durham Wasps and Humberside Hawks showed that British ice hockey is nothing if not competitive. A game between the two teams was abandoned after a mere 58 seconds when a massive punch-up broke out. Police had to step in to break up the chaos, and two Durham players were later arrested.

Dopey

The ultra-hip sport of snowboarding entered the Winter Olympics for the first time at Nagano in 1998, and ran straight into controversy. The first snowboarding gold medal winner, Canada's Ross Rebagliati, hit trouble when he was tested positive for marijuana. Rebagliati protested that he hadn't actually smoked dope for some eight months, and that the positive test came from him inhaling someone else's smoke a couple of weeks prior to the event at a going away party held in his honour. A thin excuse on the face of it maybe, but theOlympic Committee felt it was enough to let him keep the medal.

Teddy out of the pram

The American men's hockey team showed a distinct lack of sporting etiquette after their elimination from the 1998 Winter Games. Coming home without a medal, the US stars decided to partake a spot of hotel room trashing-leading to calls for them to be excluded from future Games.

FLASH
BASTARD

"HOW DO YOU PUT THESE BLOODY THINGS ON"

Triple Killy

French skier Jean-Claude Killy clinched a triple gold medal sweep of the 1968 Winter Olympics in France to please the home crowd, but it was not without controversy. Leading the slalom, Killy could only watch as first Norwegian Herbert Mjoen and then Austrian Karl Schranz both beat Killy's time, only be subsequently disqualified.

Mjoen had missed several gates on the run, but Schranz's disqualification was not so straightforward. Halfway down his run, Schranz was distracted by a French soldier who skied to close to the course. He was allowed to ski again and went faster than Killy. It turned out, though, that before falling on his first run, Schranz had already missed two gates and therefore was thrown out of the race at French insistence.

Klammer's finest moment

Franz Klammer's Olympic downhill gold medal in 1976 came thanks to a breathtaking run during which Klammer said he sacrificed safety for speed. The first part of the run was not great, he almost missed a gate early on, but the final 500 metres were vintage Klammer. "I gave myself terrible frights," the Austrian star said afterwards, "I almost fell several times. I was thrown into the air so often I was sure I was going to fall."

THEY DID IT THEIR WAY

THE 1956 WINTER GAMES WERE THE FIRST TO BE SHOWN ON TELEVISION.

Nice Little Earner

Detroit Red Wings centre Sergei Fedorov made a modest profit out of helping his team to success in the 1998 NHL. Fedorov earned a $12 million bonus for his part in the team's triumph.

"FAT MEN CAN'T JUMP" - MAGAZINE HEADLINE FOR PIECE ON THE PROPOSED COMEBACK OF EDDIE "THE EAGLE" EDWARDS.

You lose

The 1998 Stanley Cup play-offs in the American National Hockey League carried a little extra incentive. The respective state governors, John Engler of Michigan, home state of the Detroit Red Wings, an Tom Ridge of Pennsylvania, home of the Philadelphia Flyers; made a small wager on the outcome of the play-offs. The governor of the losing team would have to don the opposing team's colours and then drive the ice resurfacing machine around his home team's rink. For the record, the Red Wings won the play-offs, and Governor Tom Ridge contemplated ordering a Wings shirt in extra large.

The Eagle Lands With A Bump

Britain had a ski-jumping hero at the 1990 Winter Olympics, in the unlikely shape of a bespectacled builder called Eddie Edwards, dubbed "The Eagle", or more cruelly by an Italian journalist, a ski "dropper" rather than a jumper. Edwards became a national icon by hurtling his way down both 70 and 90 metre jumps at the Calgary games and finishing dead last. (One jumper did finish behind him, but only through disqualification).

Edwards not only made a fortune out of his antics at the Games, he also forced the Olympic Committee to make a new rule, coined the "Eddie The Eagle rule" which forces competitors to have at least some semblance of a track record in the sport.

BRITISH ICE HOCKEY CENTRE JIMMY CHAPPELL, A MEMBER OF THE VICTORIOUS BRITISH OLYMPIC SQUAD OF 1936, ALSO PLAYED FIRST CLASS CRICKET FOR CANADA.

"I WANT MY
MOMMY"

LES MENAGE A
TROIS VALLIES
TEAM

Early ice skates (the pastime dates back over 200 years in Scandinavia) were made from the rib bones of elk, ox or reindeer.

AT THE 1972 WINTER GAMES IN SAPPORO, JAPAN, MEMBERS OF THE MEDIA OUTNUMBERED ACTUAL COMPETITORS BY A RATIO OF AROUND TWO TO ONE.

Star Austrian skier Karl Schranz was expelled from the 1972 Olympics as it was deemed he was the recipient of sponsorship, thus making him a professional athlete.

THE WORLD'S FIRST SKI CLUB WAS FOUNDED IN 1861 IN NORWAY, ALTHOUGH SKI RACES OF SOME FORM WERE BEING HELD IN NORWAY AS EARLY AS THE 1760S.

> "I'VE HAD MY NOSE BROKEN, MY FACE PUNCHED IN. IF YOU CAN'T PLAY THE GAME, GO PLAY TENNIS."
> Edmonton Oiler ice hockey player Bryan Marchmont.

One of Britain's luge team members in the 1988 Winter Games was Nick Ovett, brother of top runner Steve.

COMPUTERS WERE USED FOR THE FIRST TIME AT THE 1964 WINTER GAMES TO HELP WITH JUDGING AND TIMING OF RACES.

The North American television rights for the 1988 Winter Games in Calgary, Canada, were snapped up by ABC for a cool $309 million.

SOME OF THE TEAM OFFICIALS ATTENDING THE 1988 WINTER GAMES FOUND THEIR ACCOMMODATION HAD, UNTIL VERY RECENTLY, BEEN A BROTHEL.

" I MUST LOSE WEIGHT, CAN'T SEE A BLOODY THING."

Flaming jumper

The 1994 Winter Games in Lillehammer, Norway, were opened when ski-jumper Stein Gruben demonstrated his jumping prowess while carrying the Olympic Torch to the opening ceremony. It does not record how far he actually jumped in this unofficial practice run.

Celebrity bobs

The bobsled event at the 1988 Games saw some unlikely competitors. Firstly there was a team from Jamaica (who later inspired a hit film called "Cool Running") and then there was Prince Albert of Monaco, partnering a croupier from one of Monaco's famous casinos in the two-man bob event.

"I WENT TO A FIGHT THE OTHER NIGHT AND AN ICE HOCKEY GAME BROKE OUT."
Rodney Dangerfield

THE MOMENT ALFRED HITCHCOCK GOT THE IDEA FOR THE FILM "VERTIGO."

"A PUCK IS A HARD RUBBER DISK THAT HOCKEY PLAYERS STRIKE WHEN THEY CAN'T HIT ONE ANOTHER."
Jim Cannon

"OW! YOU'VE SQUASHED A BOLLOCK DOWN TO MY KNEE!"

STILL A FLASH BASTARD

A MERE SHADOW OF HIS FORMER
SNOW-BOARDING TECHNIQUE

BRITAIN'S OLDEST SKATING ORGANISATION, THE EDINBURGH SKATING CLUB, WAS FORMED IN 1642.

FART ALERT!

ELVIS IS ALIVE!

Polished act

The Caledonian Curling Club, the international governing body of curling, was founded in 1838. It became the Royal Caledonian Curling Club four years later after an exhibition match was played for an audience consisting of Queen Victoria and Prince Albert-the match was played out on the highly polished floor of one of the Palace drawing rooms.

HE'S GOT A NICE HELMET

WOULD YOU BUY A USED SLEDGE FROM THIS LOT?

Wish I'd been there

Katarina Witt retained her figure-skating title at the 1988 Games, and also caused a stir among the judges with her taste for revealing costumes.

Not so Pally

Mark Pallister has a famous cousin,
Middlesbrough's Gary. But Mark is not
unknown in sporting circles, as an ice
hockey player with Telford Tigers. In
fact, Pallister was at one stage the
game's most penalized player, and he
has the dubious distinction of being sent
off after only 24 seconds in one game
for fighting. The skirmish had actually
broken out during the warm up!

METAL SKIS WERE USED FOR THE FIRST TIME IN ALPINE
SKIING EVENTS IN THE 1960
WINTER GAMES.

SNOW BUM

> **"IT'S HARD TO PUNISH SOMEONE MAKING $10 MILLION A YEAR. DO YOU THINK THEY REALLY CARE?"**
> American Olympic luge rider Chris Thorpe on his country's ice hockey team's antics.

> **"I'D JUST LIKE TO SAY THAT I'M SORRY I INTERFERED."**
> Ice skater Tonya Harding shows some remorse.

> **THE 1980 OLYMPIC VILLAGE AT LAKE PLACID ENDED UP BEING USED AS A PRISON.**

**"IF A GUY CAN SMOKE DOPE AND STILL GO THAT
FAST, THEY NOT ONLY SHOULD LET HIM
KEEP THE MEDAL, THEY SHOULD BUILD A STATUE OF HIM."**

Tony Kornheiser of the
Washington Post on Ross Rebagliati.

**"I'M NOT GOING TO CHANGE MY FRIENDS;
I DON'T CARE WHAT ANY OF YOU THINK ABOUT
THAT. LIFE IS AN EDUCATIONAL PROCESS. EVERYONE KNOWS YOU'RE
SUPPOSED TO WEAR A CONDOM, BUT IT DOESN'T ALWAYS HAPPEN."**

Canadian snowboarder Ross Rebagliati, tested positive for marijuana after winning
Olympic gold, shows a touch of the Eric Cantona in his press statement.

**"NOTHING PERSONAL BUT THE JETS ARE IMPORTANT. IT'S NOT AS IF
CHARLES HAS GOT DI WITH HIM."**

A drinker at Bailey's Bar in Winnipeg gives his reason for watching the Jets play
their last ice hockey game at Manitoba rather than join the crowds at the visit
of Prince Charles on the same day.

"WHY COULDN'T WE FLY HERE LIKE EVERYONE ELSE?"

1956 WINTER GAMES FIGURE-SKATING CHAMPION TENLEY ALBRIGHT SUFFERED FROM POLIO AS A CHILD.

"KIDS KNOW THE RULES; WOMEN KNOW THE RULES; BASICALLY, YOUR DOG KNOWS THE RULES."
Canadian ice hockey player Ken Priestlay explains how popular the game is in his home country.

"IF AMERICA CAN FORGIVE MIKE TYSON FOR RAPING A WOMAN, WHY IN GOD'S NAME CAN'T TONYA HARDING RETURN TO FIGURE SKATING?"
Tonya Harding's agent, David Hans Schmidt.

"OOUU! WHO DROPPED THAT ONE."

V sign

Sweden's Jan Boklev revolutionised the ski jump in 1988 by jumping with his skis making the shape of a 'V' through the air rather than maintaining the traditional parallel position. Boklev was initially penalized for the new style, but it has since become the norm among jumpers.

"THEY'LL PROBABLY SIT WHERE THE REST OF THEM ARE - IN MY MOM'S DRESSER, COLLECTING DUST. GOLD, SILVER, AND BRONZE ISN'T SPECIAL. IT'S GIVING 100 PER CENT AND KNOWING YOU'VE DONE THE BEST YOU CAN."
Speed-skater Eric Heiden after winning five gold medals at the 1980 Olympics.

THERE IS EVIDENCE POINTING TO THE FACT THAT THE WORLD'S FIRST SKIERS WERE HITTING THE PISTES SOME 3000 YEARS BEFORE THE BIRTH OF CHRIST.

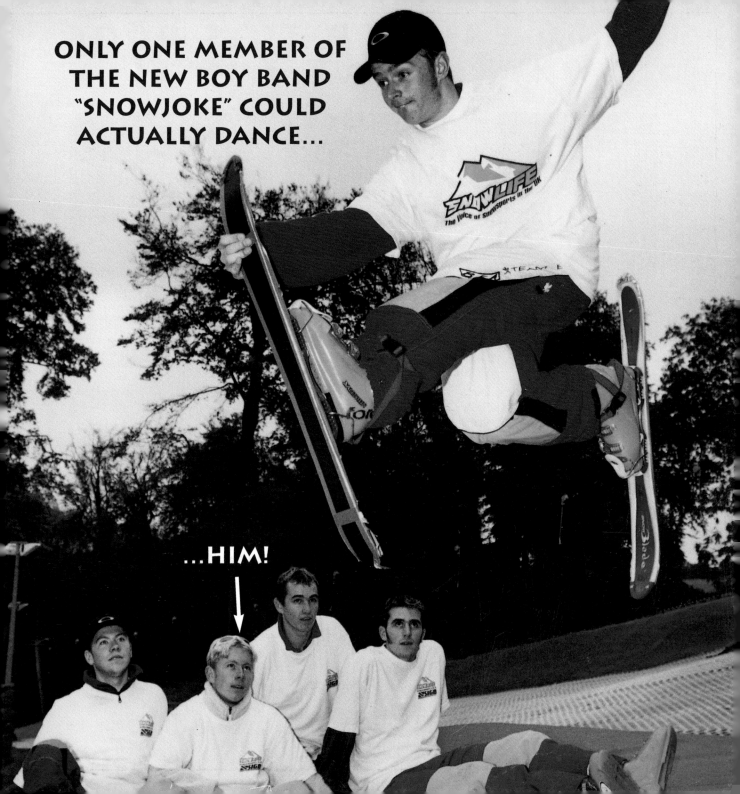

IF YOU ENJOYED THIS BOOK, WHAT ABOUT THESE!

All these books are available at your local book shop or can be ordered direct from the publisher.

Just list the titles you require and give your name address, including postcode.

Prices and availability are subject to change without notice.

Please send to Chameleon Cash Sales, 76 Dean Street, London W1V 5HA, a cheque or postal order for £7.99 and add the following for postage and packaging:

UK - £1.00 For the first book, 50p for the second and 30p for the third and for each additional book up to a maximum of £3.00.

OVERSEAS - (including Eire) £2.00 For the first book, £1.00 for the second and 50p for each additional book up to a maximum of £3.00.